Somewhere In Between

Somewhere In Between

The Hokey Pokey, Chocolate Cake, and The Shared Death Experience

By Lizzy Miles

Trail Angel Press
Columbus

Published by Trail Angel Press

ISBN-10: 1937574024
ISBN-13: 978-1937574024

Designed by Lizzy Miles
Edited by James Miles
Title by Don "The Idea Guy" Snyder

This book is dedicated to all of my guardian angels,
but especially the one who helps me find
the good parking spaces

Contents

Introduction

Before I get to the heart of my storytelling, I do think it would be helpful for you to have some context for the stories and how I came to work with the dying. When I tell people that I work in hospice, I often hear, "it takes a special person." I think that everyone is special and everyone has the ability to be present with the dying. Most just do not want to think about death or dying. I became comfortable being with the dying through experience. Many people who work in the field of death and dying will tell you that they didn't choose the career, it chose them. I have experienced a wide variety of losses and have shed my share of tears. When I reached double digit losses, however, something clicked inside. I stopped counting losses and started counting guardian angels. Maybe I got tired of crying, but I figured I might as well embrace the impermanence of it all. I still cry, but I have learned to laugh too. I believe that the full expression of emotions helps us to work through our grief, whether we are grieving for those who have died or those who will die. This is harsh, but it is important to realize that we are all going to die someday. Look, I don't want to sound like a Hallmark card, but it is true that each day is precious. Live it up. Laugh. Love life. My hope for this book is that my stories bring you comfort and perhaps make you smile. You are stronger than you know.

Now for my background. First and foremost, I am a third-generation believer in the metaphysical. I grew up with pyramids around my house. I remember my grandmother reading palms and talking about reincarnation. She was actively involved in the Rosicrucian Order. Most of my family members on my dad's side were strongly influenced by her beliefs, including my dad, his sister and myself. As a child, when I would ask my parents, "What religion are we?" the response was *we are all religions*. While this was somewhat confusing to me as a child, I am now okay with not categorizing my belief system. Indeed, as I learn more about Christianity, Buddhism, Hinduism and Judaism, I see the similarities between the doctrines, rather than the differences. To borrow from the Dali Lama, *my religion is kindness.*

My father was in the military and I lived half of my childhood overseas. Although I was born in Omaha, I only lived there for three months and continued to move frequently for the rest of my childhood. I lived in Okinawa, Turkey, Puerto Rico, the Philippines and Germany. I strongly believe the frequent relocations shaped who I am today. With overseas military dependents, there is an understanding of a shared experience that defines our core. We learned early in our lives that nothing was permanent. We understood loss, as we were constantly saying goodbye. While that may seem sad, it was actually liberating. We learned to change our friends, our environment and ourselves. As we lost old friends, we made new ones. Most military dependents have learned to be highly adaptable, by necessity.

To establish stability for me because we were moving a lot, my parents shared parenting of me with my Aunt Jerry and Uncle Paul. I lived with my aunt and uncle off and on several times while growing up and even attended school while I was with them. For this reason, they are like my second parents. Having two sets of parents was both a blessing and a curse. Because my parents were so completely different from my aunt and uncle in child-rearing philosophies, I often found myself in conflict with one set of 'parents' immediately after the transitions. My parents were hands-off and my aunt and uncle were hands-on. My mother certainly did not appreciate the comparisons when I would tell her that my aunt did things a different way. This struggle between the two worlds forced me to learn flexibility and adaptability.

My undergraduate focus in school was Communication. I wanted to ultimately get my doctorate, but when I graduated I ended up working in a medical records department for the local cancer hospital. As I analyzed the records, I came to understand how much the physicians truly cared for their patients and the work that they do. I went on to work in health care survey research where I read thousands of patient comments about their hospital or outpatient experience. I learned from these patient comments that sometimes the simplest act of kindness from a medical staff member can yield immense gratitude. I learned that the patients' overall impressions of their hospital stay were most closely tied to their experiences with their nurse. Physicians who sat down were perceived to have spent more time with the patient. Nobody liked hospital food. While I enjoyed the work, the pace of the growing company was exhausting and like many offices ours had its share of politics, and eventually I left.

Somehow, following the wind, I ended up working in retail marketing. I was at a good company, and I stayed there for a long time, but I never felt that I belonged. Anxious to get back to health care, I returned to school while I was still working and I received my Master's in Journalism and Communication with a focus on health communication. I graduated and nothing happened. I guess I thought clouds would part and I would see a beam of light directing me which way to go.

My mom was in declining health and living in an assisted living facility, and while I cannot say I was the best daughter that I wish I would have been, thoughts of her consumed my day. I did not worry so much about my career. In the final days before she died, I felt that I did the best that I could and ultimately her death was peaceful.

A few years and a few more family deaths later, I decided to start volunteering for a hospice. I volunteered for a couple of years and loved it so much that I decided I wanted to work in hospice. I researched the hospice careers and determined that I was not strong enough in the sciences to become a nurse, so I returned to school yet again to get a master's degree in social work.

The stories contained in this book are all true experiences I have had in my journeys with dying patients, including my own family members and other friends I have made along the way.

Aunt Jerry and
Our Shared Death Experience

It was April, 2010 and I was in my final quarter of my master's program in social work when I received the dreaded phone call. It was my Uncle Paul and he calmly told me, "Aunt Jerry is in the hospital, she's had two seizures and a heart attack."

I expected him to follow that sentence with the news that she had died, but he did not. He told me she was in the emergency room and was going to be admitted to the hospital. My Aunt Jerry was my dad's last living sibling and his baby sister. She was also like a second mom to me, as I had lived with my aunt and uncle several times while growing up.

My aunt and uncle lived in Cleveland, Ohio which is about two hours from Columbus, where I live. In 2009, they celebrated their fiftieth wedding anniversary. They had 3 and ½ daughters, Jerri Lynn, Cathy, Paula and myself.

My Aunt Jerry was adventurous and loved life. She traveled to six continents. She was a pilot. She drove boats. She played golf. My uncle said that if you had adventurous feminist on one side, and traditional female on the other, my aunt straddled the line straight down the middle.

She was the one who taught me to drive – first a golf cart in Puerto Rico when I was 10, and then a car when I came back to the United States at 17. She taught me to cook and plan ahead for parties. Unlike my parents, she made me make my bed and eat Brussels sprouts. She always asked me how my day was and she liked to sing and she loved to laugh.

At the time of this phone call, my aunt was also in the late stages of Alzheimer's disease. She was formally diagnosed with Alzheimer's in 1997, but my uncle suspects that there were signs of it years earlier when she had trouble remembering how to play bridge. My uncle cared for his beloved wife for as long as he could at home, but as the disease progressed, he found he needed help. In 2004, he moved her to Kemper House, an Alzheimer's facility in Cleveland. He visited her almost every day and over the six years she was there, he would come to know all of the staff and most of the residents and their families. He was as involved as a caregiver could be.

Shared Death Experience

So what is a Shared Death Experience (SDE)? The term was coined by Raymond Moody, the same researcher who coined the phrase Near Death Experience also known as NDE. A Near Death Experience happens when someone dies for a brief period of time and experiences unusual events of a metaphysical nature such as seeing a tunnel, spirits, heaven or a light. When the person is revived or comes back to life on their own, these experiences stay with them and often profoundly change their outlook on life.

The Shared Death Experience has also been known as "empathetic NDE", "conjoint NDE" or "mutual NDE." The concept of an SDE is that a person experiences some of what the dying person does, but is not dying themselves. It is not a new phenomenon, but it is not as well known or as well understood as the NDE. In part, the mystery is because people who have these SDE experiences are reluctant to talk about them, for fear of the reactions of others.

The book *Glimpses of Eternity* by Raymond Moody, about shared death experiences, was published in October 2010, and I discovered it in May of 2011. One year to the month after my aunt died, I came across this book and finally realized that there was a *name* for the phenomenon I had experienced. I had not previously made the connection with nor identified with the NDE community, but when I discovered this book it was an emotional moment for me. I was validated, and I realized that I was not alone in my experiences.

As I mentioned previously, I have always been a believer in the metaphysical world. I feel it is important to relay that I personally had never had a metaphysical experience prior to this point. I was not psychic. Everything that happened at my aunt's bedside was completely new and confusing to me. I am not sure I have even fully processed the entire experience, but perhaps telling the story is in itself part of the processing.

Timing – Messages from God

I drove up to Cleveland the evening that I got the phone call that my aunt was in the hospital. When I arrived at Southwest General hospital, several family members were sitting around my aunt's bed. She was hooked up to a heart monitor, had a saline IV, and was on oxygen. Her eyes were closed. I pulled up a chair and sat at her feet. I closed my eyes and began to pray. Mostly I was asking God for a peaceful transition. I felt I really could not hope for anything more than that.

It was not very long before I started to see amazing swirls of colors in my head. I had never seen colors so vivid before. These were colors that you cannot find in the Crayola box. The first color started as a red spot and then it floated and evolved, swirling and changing into other colors – oranges, blues, purples and then white. I started to feel light headed, and I felt as if my body were swaying back and forth like I was on a boat. It was disorienting. I felt as if someone or something was pulling me from the top of my head. The only thing I can compare it to would be perhaps weightlessness in a fast moving elevator. Then in my mind's eye, I saw a tunnel. There was a shadow of a person who just said *"Jerry, we're here whenever you're ready."* Then I felt sheer and complete panic and heaviness, and all the colors and pictures in my head were gone. I snapped back to the hospital room in a thud. I opened my eyes and everything was the same in the room, but I was different. I looked at my Aunt Jerry and she had her eyes closed. I had no idea that this was just the beginning or what the next 12 days would bring.

Given her condition at the time of her admission to the hospital, I was surprised that my aunt made it through the night. Not only did she survive the first night and the one after that, but we were able to get her discharged to hospice back at Kemper House, the Alzheimer's facility where she lived. The facility was gracious and allowed us to stay and I ended up staying overnight there in the facility, along with my cousin Jerri Lynn who had come from Connecticut and my uncle. My uncle did not want to leave my aunt's side.

I believe it was the day after discharge where I had my second vision related to timing. I saw the backyard of my aunt's and my dad's childhood home, and there were a crowd of people standing there. I could not make out faces but I sensed they were family. They just simply said, *"We're all here for you Jerry."*

Perhaps three days after she was discharged at the hospital, we were all surprised that she was still living since she was not taking in any food or water. I saw the same group of people in the backyard. It was the same scene as before, and they said, *"we're all here for you."* But this time they pulled up chairs and were sitting down and they said, in almost a resigned sort of way, *"This is going to take a while."* My cousin Jerri Lynn was the only one who was open to hearing what I was experiencing, and I passed on to her what I had learned. After that vision, I knew my aunt was not going anywhere anytime soon.

Later that week, my dad arrived in town from Europe and told me that he had meditated on the situation of her extended dying. He told me that their four siblings in heaven were on the other side debating who was going to come to get her and in what order. He said that they kept changing sides and could not make up their collective mind. My dad did not know this, but what he was describing on the heavenly realm paralleled what was happening here on earth with my aunt. My cousins and their dad were constantly switching sides of the bed, as the side my aunt was facing was generally considered to be the preferential spot.

My father and I were at a rest stop on our way back to Columbus, and I had just come out of the restroom when I saw him in my car talking to himself. I asked him what he was doing and he said he had meditated and told the siblings to just hurry up and be on with it and relieve my aunt from her suffering. I laid down in the car to go to sleep and within just a few minutes I had another strong sensation of being out of my body. Instead of the usual floating feeling, this time it was as if someone was pulling me upside down and water was running up my nose. It was quite unpleasant and unsettling, and I sat up in the car with a start. I blamed my dad and he laughed. Again, I felt my aunt's sheer panic. From this situation, I gathered that those on the other side were becoming more persistent in trying to coax my aunt along on her journey to the other side. If they could not get her soul out through her head, why not try the feet?

Timing – Messages from My Aunt

In addition to sensing the spirit communications *to* my aunt, I also seemed to get messages *from* her as to why she could not go. And she had all kinds of reasons. Since my aunt was in the late stages of Alzheimer's, she had not been verbal for several years. All of the messages that I am about to describe came to me telepathically from my aunt.

The first reason really is not anything I heard her say but rather her reaction to the spirit leaving the body. I had that lightheaded feeling a few times and it would always end like a snapping rubber band. At the time, I wondered if it was my own panic because I did not want to actually cross that line and go to the other side, but after reflecting on it in hindsight, I believe it was her fear and panic that I was feeling, not my own.

The first couple of days back at Kemper house from the hospital, there were several cousins visiting from out of town. I received this communication from my aunt that was something along the lines of, *"It's so rare for the whole family to be together...if I die now, you will all just go home and everybody will go back to their normal lives."*

My aunt had a point. Many families who end up living in different cities only get together for weddings and funerals and ours had become that way as well. In our childhood, all of the cousins would get together at grandma's house. Once grandma died in 1981, we always meant to get together more often, but we never did.

Another time, I saw my middle cousin Cathy and her mom and I saw a really strong green aura. I sensed that my aunt was really worried about Cathy and was trying to heal her. Cathy was the daughter who had visited her mom the most, even after her mom was in the late stages of Alzheimer's and no longer recognized her. After my aunt died, Cathy had vivid dreams of her mom coming to visit her and providing healing energy.

The message that most conveys my aunt's personality and independent spirit happened when I was in another room and I got a call from a cousin who said, "THIS IS IT... SHE is GOING. Come quickly." I rushed back to the room and joined the prayer vigil around the bedside. After about ten minutes, my cousin Cathy stood up and said, "I don't think she's going to die right now. I am going to go get my hair cut." I could not believe that my cousin was going to walk away. I thought to myself that she was just overcome with the emotion of the situation and needed to get away.

Later I found out that my cousin actually HEARD her mom's voice in her head say, *"I don't know what you all are doing, I'm not going anywhere right now!"*

When my aunt was in the hospital, my dad was in Spain. Unfortunately, it was around the time of the Iceland volcano eruption in 2010, and flights were messed up. He had taken a military hop there, so if he were to try to fly commercial back it would be $5,000 each for both him and my stepmom. Fortunately, they found a military flight into Pennsylvania, but it was a planes, trains and automobiles exercise to get him back to Cleveland to see his sister. The whole family seemed to have an idea that **he** was the reason she was still alive. She must be waiting on him, we thought. Well, he got to the facility at 3:00 in the morning and spent some time with her, but then I got the message from her, *"I can't die now, everyone will think I was waiting on him, and my husband will take it personally."*

This was the last direct message that I had from her or the spirits regarding timing. Ultimately, she lived for 14 days without food, water or saline. Even though I had some insight into the timing, I still found when I reflected later that there was still so much that I did not know as evidenced by some of the old text messages and emails I sent.

4/23 [The day she went into the hospital] email to my stepmom: *Aunt Jerry in er...personally I don't think she will survive weekend*

4/25 text to my cousin: *IMHO Aunt Jerry waiting for my dad*

4/26 email to my stepmom: *she is very close...but I think if is meant to be she will wait*

4/30 email to professor: *I do not know when she is going to die... we thought she wouldn't make it out of the hospital on Sunday, and yet, here we are on Friday living minute by minute. I have been asked to write the obituary and also a memorial speech at her funeral*

5/4 email to friend: *My aunt is still with us way beyond what was expected and strangely enough it is as if her Alzheimer's has almost disappeared. This is a gift. Unfortunately...as time moves on and we have said multiple goodbyes, the family stress level increases*

From my experience with my aunt, I have expanded my personal outlook on the timing of death. There was not just one thing or one person that she needed to feel comfortable leaving - there were so many different factors at play. It reminded me of the dinner parties she hosted and all of the components that needed to be in place before the guests arrived: appetizers...check, table set...check, wine chilled... check. I would like to think that she was preparing the ultimate party up in heaven.

The negotiation between my aunt and the spirits fascinates me. I have seen it happen several times. Even in patients that are no longer able to talk, I've seen them sort of sleep-talking and there is definitely listening and then talking, or negotiating. This ongoing conversation with God can last weeks, if not longer.

Spirit Communication

All of the timing visions and spirit communication that I experienced so far, I had my eyes closed. However, I had some spirit contact with my eyes open.

Before this experience, I wanted to see spirits. I begged for it. WHY? I am a believer, why can't I see spirits? Then once I got the ability to sense spirit activity it scared me. Once I turned it on, I could not turn it off. I do not see people shapes. I just see sparks. They look like the sparks you see when someone is flicking a lighter. They are there and then gone. They zip around the room and when my aunt was dying they were *in the room* constantly.

My cousin Jerri Lynn and I were sitting on each side of my aunt, and I kept seeing sparks behind her. I told her and she said she thought she felt something too. She said, "let's close our eyes and see if we can figure it out." So we closed our eyes, and in less than two minutes, my cousin starting laughing out loud. I told her that I did not work that fast and I needed more time. Eventually I just got this strong knowing that my uncle's brother Rick, who had died many years ago, was in the room. We thought that made sense, since stories of Rick had kept coming up previously that day.

Then I asked my cousin what made her laugh and she told me that she actually heard our grandmother's voice in her head clear as day, *"let Elizabeth figure it out for herself."*

That night when we tried to go to sleep, both my cousin and I were feeling unsettled by the spirit activity in the room. Even though we knew the spirits were likely to be family, there was something freaky about that halfway connection of seeing stuff flying around the room when we did not know exactly who was there. I still do see sparks occasionally now, but it is never when I am *trying* to see them.

Pain Control

There is a hypothetical question – if you were a super hero, what super powers would you like to have? The ability to fly? X-ray vision? An alternative question is: if you were psychic, what psychic powers would you like to have? Would you like to be able to see the future? Talk to spirits? I have always been an empathetic person, but I had never been able to actually feel someone else's physical pain until this event. AND I would not wish that ability on anyone.

The first time I felt her pain was when we were in the hospital room and I lost circulation in my legs. Weird things happened with my body a few times before I decided that indeed it was my aunt's pain I was feeling and not my own. I confirmed it when I would go up to her and see her facial grimaces and would ask my uncle about her last medication administration. The most common pain of hers I felt was a heaviness in my chest and difficulty breathing.

I received validation for myself of my ability to channel her pain when I had gone home to Columbus for a day to get more clothes, six days after her original hospital admission. I was lying in bed, and my left shoulder randomly started hurting. The next day I spoke with my cousin who was still in Cleveland, and she confirmed that at the time my shoulder was hurting, my aunt appeared to be uncomfortable lying on her side. Jerri Lynn told me that she had wanted to reposition my aunt but my uncle overruled her request.

Unfortunately, I found *myself* at odds with my uncle several times over my aunt's pain management. Like many family members in this situation, my uncle was reluctant to have my aunt receive morphine. He did not want her to be "drugged up" but also there was an attempt to control the process. And did I mention that he has a PhD in Analytical Chemistry? Imagine *his* reaction when I (his *niece*) would try to give him direction on how to administer medication. Because I would see and *feel* my aunt's pain, and because I knew about pain control from my hospice experience, it was even more stressful for me.

One day I called one of my co-workers back home in tears. Shellie was a hospice nurse. I told her that I could not stand that my aunt was suffering because my uncle was restricting the dosage. She told me, "Elizabeth, Your aunt and uncle have been married for FIFTY years. This journey is about them." She also told me that if my aunt was suffering because of my uncle, "she'll just let him have it in the afterlife." I tried to listen to her and it helped for a few days, but my aunt was the one who was sharing her pain with me.

One night I could not sleep so I left the room and called my cousin Sally who worked 3rd shift as a nurse. We talked for about an hour and then got disconnected. I called her back, we talked for five minutes and got disconnected again. I called her back a third time and we joked that if we got disconnected one more time, then it was a sign. Well, we were disconnected again. At that point, I felt I needed to go back to the room. I walked into the room and my aunt's eyes were wide open, staring at me. I went to her bedside and she clutched my hand tightly. Everything about her screamed PAIN. I woke my uncle up who was a little groggy and told him she needed morphine. Not one to take someone else's word for it, he had to ask her himself. He said, "Jerry, squeeze my hand if you need some medicine." She squeezed it tightly so he conceded and gave her 10 milligrams of the morphine.

I went to sleep in the corner of the room and woke up around 5:45 a.m. with chest pain and shortness of breath. I went up to my aunt and once again, her face was wincing, her eyes were wide open and she grabbed by hand. I woke up my uncle and told him that she needed some morphine.

He said "she feels relaxed to me."

I said "she is *squeezing* my hand."

He said, "the nurse would be here in about a half hour."

This went on for several minutes and I finally pleaded, "PLEASE Uncle Paul, just come to this side and **look** at **her** face."

He replied shortly and sternly, "This… is… NOT… a….negotiation!"

My eyes welled up in tears. **Just then**, the aides came in. I stood up, threw my hands down in disgust and yelled, "She's in PAIN. Just LOOK at her" and stomped out of the room. I walked around the corner, and saw my cousin Cathy walking towards me, having just arrived from home. She looked at my face and immediately I knew she was interpreting my expression as an indication that her mom had died. I shook my head no and yelled something about her dad and went stomping and swearing down the hallway of the facility. The last time I lived with my aunt and uncle, I was 17. At that moment, I was 17 again.

My uncle ended up following me and we sat down for a bit. He seemed to understand my stress but justified his actions by explaining that he knew the nurse was coming shortly. I calmed down and we went back towards the room and found that the aides were still there. My uncle saw the nurse in the hallway and casually suggested that a dose of morphine might be needed. She asked how much and he said 10mg. I was standing behind him with my thumbs up in the air indicating HIGHER. When the nurse returned to the room with the morphine, she said, "Ok so we're going to give her 15 mg."

My uncle was confused. "Uhhh, I said 10." The nurse told him that 15 would probably be better because the aides had indicated she was unsettled by the changing and turning and he conceded.

When my uncle left the room, I approached my Aunt Jerry and told her in an even firm tone, "Aunt Jerry, I love that you have given me the ability to hear you, but you can't ever do that to me again. You *know* I can't stand up to him. You know he scares me." My aunt indicated with her eyes a slightly guilty expression as if to say, "I know, I know. I know that was not fair, but I was desperate." After that, she took to calling my cousin Jerri Lynn by making her think that she left something in the room. My cousin would walk into the room, find her mom in pain and then convince her dad to give her mom the morphine.

When the hospice nurse came the following day, I told her about some of the pain control issues, and she was able to educate my uncle a little bit more about how to better treat my aunt's symptoms. My uncle was, and has always been, a very orderly and precise man. The dying process, however, is anything *but* orderly and precise.

Life Review

Feeling my aunt's pain and dealing with pain control issues was perhaps one of the worst parts of the experience... but one of the best parts was what I believe to be her sharing parts of her life review with me.

When I would try to go to sleep, I would often see the colors that I had mentioned earlier. One night when I closed my eyes, I saw a moving picture of an amusement park ride. It was round and spinning. It was in full color and I was awake... it was as if I was watching TV with my eyes closed. I had never visualized something so clearly, so I knew that it was related to my aunt.

I did not know how to broach the subject, so the next day, I just asked my cousin Cathy if my aunt ever went to amusement parks. It was, in my opinion, a rather dumb question because there is a major amusement park right near Cleveland, but I did not know how else to ask.

My cousin's response was, "Yes, but she didn't like the roller coaster, she liked the rides that went around…they made her laugh."

No matter how many times my experiences and visions were validated, each new validation would surprise me. This was no exception. I found myself seeking out the visions but I never seemed to be able to control when they happened. Most of the time, they would happen when I was trying to go to sleep at the end of a long, mentally exhausting day. I would close my eyes and then the colors or movies would start.

The next time I saw a movie in my head I saw a red convertible with four people in it – two guys and two girls. I remember the girl in the backseat had medium length blond hair and they were waving their arms around and laughing, and I like to think of it as, "up to no good."

I approached my uncle gingerly. He was not the type to believe in any of this sort of thing. I said, "I had a dream… does a red convertible mean anything to you and Aunt Jerry?"

And he said, "Yes! My brother Rick had a convertible and we went on double dates in it."

Ohhh. Really cool. I felt validated. I told him that I had seen an amusement park ride earlier and asked him if he wanted me to continue to share the pictures that I saw. He said that he did not think so. At some point I believe he conveyed that he did not understand why the rest of us were communicating with her in a way that he could not. They were married, after all, for 50 years.

The final scene that I saw was the longest. Again, it was when I was trying to go to sleep. I felt like I was young. I was riding in something and facing backwards… watching the landscape go by.. rolling green hills… it went on for quite a while. It was very peaceful. Because I felt young, I asked my dad what it was from… he tried to find significance based on a fable (*Perhaps it's the fable about the Turkish man who rides the donkey backwards?*). I was very insistent that it was definitely a memory of my aunt's.

Then it came to him. When they were in elementary school and their father was still alive, once a year the family would drive from Dayton to Oxford, Ohio. In Oxford, their dad would empty one of the penny vending machines that he owned. My dad said that he had fond memories of those trips because everyone would be together, and they would have sandwiches and would get to keep the dimes that people had dropped in the penny machines. My dad confirmed for me that my aunt always liked to ride in the back of the truck.

Synchronicities

The final component of this experience that I want to share with you is some of the synchronicities that happened. I have been blogging about synchronicities for seven years. Oftentimes, the meaning behind the coincidence is only significant to the person experiencing the synchronicities. In my experience each individual synchronicity is ambiguous, but when you look at them in groups and over time as the volume of them increases, they are more startling. I would highly encourage you to journal your coincidences.

There were several times during the week where I felt guided by forces beyond my understanding, and meaningful coincidences happened. Here are just a few examples.

- The room next to my aunt was empty and I ran in there to use the bathroom. There was an activities employee who was just in there for a second, and we started talking. Somehow we got on the subject of metaphysical things and he told me about a Goddess Elite metaphysical store. I needed to get away for a little bit, so I decided to go.

- I plugged the address into my GPS and found that when I got there, it was down the street from where I had lived with my aunt and uncle when I was 17.

- I came across puzzle charms that I adored. The display showed charms with 30-40 different sayings but in the case there were only four left. At first I was disappointed that I did not get to choose which saying, but then I realized that the messages on the four charms that were left seemed to coincide with my cousins and myself. I felt I needed to buy them. Two said *I am perfect health* (I knew my cousin had knee surgery, but I did not know my other cousin was having health issues as well). One said *I am optimistic* (totally me) and one *I am original* (100% Jerri Lynn).

- There were some pretty blue bracelets on sale and I felt a strong compulsion to buy a large handful of them. I was not sure why. Later, the tension started to increase with my cousins and I just knew that I was supposed to pass them out. I gave one to all the women in the family and put one on my aunt's wrist. It reminded us that we were all connected, and it seemed to bring peace for a little while.

T.J.Maxx

You might be amused that all of my synchronicities are related to shopping. I swear I do not shop that much, really! I went to T.J.Maxx to get more clothes because I had only packed a few outfits and I did not want to drive back to Columbus. When I was at the store, I came across a book called *Future Lives* by Gloria Chadwick. This book is not your typical T.J.Maxx fare – they do not sell many books, and they do not generally carry metaphysical books. This book was synchronous to me in two ways. First, inside the book there was an extended twenty page meditation which reflected my color visions exactly. It was as if the author was witnessing what I saw and describing it. Second, I believe I was guided to buy the book by and for my aunt. Perhaps she knew that we were struggling about what to do at the bedside. The thought occurred to me to read from the book to her. My aunt visibly relaxed when anyone read to her from this book.

Additionally, I am a little embarrassed to be writing about my underwear but there is a synchronicity with it as well. I had to buy more underwear because I had stayed longer than I had originally expected to stay. I came across underwear by the brand name *Itsy Bitsy* which was freakishly close to my aunt and uncle's childhood nickname for me of *Itsybits*. A year later, I inadvertently packed this same underwear for my trip to Miami where I was presenting this story at a conference. I wore that underwear the day I presented, but I did not share the underwear synchronicity with my audience. The cliché is that the *speaker* is supposed to picture the *audience* in their underwear, not the other way around.

Candy

Near the beginning of my visit, when I ran an errand to the grocery store, I found myself drawn to the bulk candy aisle. I like candy but like most people, I try to watch what I buy. For some reason though, I felt compelled to buy large quantities of candy. I bought candy I did not even like. I bought more candy than I could ever imagine anyone would eat. I really could not help myself and I did not know why.

Later, when I was talking to my cousin about it, she reminded me that our grandfather's job was a candy and nuts distributer and that my dad and my aunts grew up with pounds of candy in the house. The love of candy has been passed down through the generations. Maybe I subconsciously knew that or maybe the spirits guided me. I do not know. What I do know is that my family members LOVED digging through the candies looking for their favorites and reminiscing, and it seemed to provide a glimpse of happy in a sad situation.

The Dates

There seemed to be an unavoidable synchronicity with dates. Two of my cousins and myself all had May birthdays and just to torment, throw Mother's Day into the timeframe as well. When we were trying to anticipate when my aunt would die, it was if there was a ball on a roulette wheel spinning… my cousins did not want her to die on their birthday or mother's day or have the funeral on their birthday or mother's day. Well, with two birthdays within the same week, that did not leave a lot of days available. My aunt died on the day of her youngest child's 44th birthday. The following year, 2011, on her birthday my cousin Paula had a double-whammy of the anniversary of her mother's death and Mother's Day. Whether it is ironic or a synchronicity, Paula was the cousin who had the hardest time with the situation while her mother was dying.

You may be surprised to know that I chose to leave Cleveland and return to Columbus before my aunt passed. I had put my life on hold and it was starting to take its toll on me. I also felt that my presence, while welcome, was also that of an enabler. I felt that I had done my part and that I needed to step back. I left Cleveland on May 4th. My aunt died on May 8, 2010.

After the Funeral

The Penny Cross

My cousin Jerri Lynn had a friend from England who also happened to be psychic. The friend gave my cousin some messages about my aunt and mentioned that she was buried with a cross. My cousin Jerri Lynn told the psychic that she was mistaken. My aunt was not Catholic and was not buried with a cross. The psychic was adamant that she was. Jerri Lynn mentioned the discussion to me and that she did not know why the psychic was saying that. I happened to mention it to my dad when I was talking to him on the phone and then there was silence. He then admitted that he had a tiny copper cross that was cut out of a penny and had slipped it into the casket for his sister. It was his little secret between him and his sister, or so he thought. The news that the psychic had insisted that she was buried with a cross was comforting to him, as it was a bit of confirmation that the cross was noticed. I called my cousin Jerri Lynn back and let her know about my dad's shenanigans.

The Letter

Three days before the one year anniversary of my aunt's death, the Cleveland Alzheimer's Association had their annual dinner. My uncle invited me to attend the event. When I called to say I was 20 minutes away, he told me that he would be in the shower and I was to let myself in and make myself comfortable.

When I got to his house, I immediately went to the bookcase. He has floor to ceiling books about 20 feet across with a big ladder. It is my dream library! The second book I picked up, *Messages from the Masters*, had a "Dear Diary" letter written on loose-leaf notebook paper by my aunt in 1969. It was filled front and back, and she wrote about her strong desire to have a 4th child, but only if it were a boy. She relayed a conversation that she had with my uncle about the decision whether or not they were going to have another child.

Even though all I had done was open a book, I felt as if I had been snooping. I put the letter back in the book and back on the bookshelf. I did not tell my uncle about it and we went to the dinner.

After the evening was over and we were sitting at the kitchen table sharing memories, I decided to tell him about the letter. He had never seen it before and obviously had no idea that it existed. He read it over a couple of times and then leaned back in his chair and contemplated the implications. "I never knew she felt that way" he said more than once, and he talked to me about that time in their marriage.

A month later, I was on the phone with him and he mentioned the letter again. I believe in my heart that my aunt guided me to find that letter and give it to him.

Pictures

Mid-May in the year following her death, I emailed my uncle a list of pictures that I would like to have for my presentation about the experience at the Association for Death Education annual conference in Miami. He said he had thousands of pictures and they were all over, but he would do his best to look through and try to get me the pictures that I wanted.

A week passed and I had not heard back from him. Even though I had a friend from out of town and other deadlines, the thought occurred to me that I should go see him. I asked if it would be alright if I could drive up and go through the pictures myself. He said yes and gave me several days that he was available.

I picked a Monday. I did not realize that I picked the day of their wedding anniversary. He told me about halfway through the day that it was their anniversary and said that I provided a helpful distraction from his grief. We talked about my bedside experience with my aunt and everything that happened. I talked about the presentation I was about to give. He did not remember our "standoff" over pain control at all but said that the conversation did sound like him.

He still did not understand how or why my aunt had communicated with me and not him. Nor did he understand how my cousin Cathy can have vivid dreams about my aunt and he does not or how my cousin Jerri Lynn can see signs and he does not. Yet, I believe it was for him that my aunt directed me to the letter, and I believe she directed me to visit on their anniversary.

Part II

Other Tales from the Bedside

Perhaps the Hokey Pokey Is
What It's All About

It was a Friday night when I received a call from my Uncle Paul who told me that my Aunt Jerry, who had end-stage Alzheimer's disease, had suffered two seizures and a heart attack and was in the hospital. With her condition, one might have expected that she might have died the next day. She did not. She lived for another two weeks without food, water or saline IV.

As much as we expect that we will do bedside vigil in someone's last minutes, the truth of the matter is that sometimes the minutes stretch to hours, which stretch to days, which stretch to weeks. At least, that is what happened to us. It was and is impossible to live in a state of crisis for an extended period of time. We tried to make sense of why we were there for such a long time, but we surprised ourselves and ultimately found a way to cope with our grief by singing.

When it was just my cousin Jerri Lynn, the oldest daughter, and myself in the room, we did what we could to keep the energy light. One time when my uncle left for a few hours, he put Jerri Lynn in charge. She turned to her mom (my aunt) and said, "Dad's gone, now we can dance!"

As she said that, she made a big sweeping gesture with her arm and I asked her if she was doing the "Hokey Pokey." Since my aunt had been in and out and up and down so many times over the past few weeks, we felt somehow as if it was a great metaphor for her transition.

Jerri Lynn started it with her right arm. You put your right arm in, you put your right arm out. We made it through several body parts before the aides walked in the room. They were quite surprised when they saw us doing the "Hokey Pokey," but I think it was good for them. One of them even joined us for a few rounds, albeit reluctantly. Jerri Lynn and I tried to keep the energy the way my aunt would have wanted it. She always had a smile on her face. She loved to giggle. What better way to honor her than to do the "Hokey Pokey" with her?

The "Hokey Pokey" sparked something in us, and my cousin and I then reminisced about the songs that my aunt had sung to us as children. Jerri Lynn sang the lullaby that her mom had sung to her and that our grandmother had sung to our parents. Jerri Lynn sang the lullaby over and over and every time she did, we could see the tension release in my aunt's face (and ours too). It was a song based upon a poem written by my grandmother that has special meaning for the whole family.

We even recalled my aunt's wake-up song. Imagine being a teenager trying to sleep in, and your mom/aunt comes barging in the room singing some perky pick up song, "RISE and SHINE and give GOD your glory, glory!" Well, we sang that song too.

As my other cousins came in and found us singing, they would join in. Later there was a chorus of her daughters and myself singing the childhood song, "Boom Boom Ain't it Great to be Crazy?" That song was a stress-reliever for sure, even if we couldn't remember all of the words.

Perhaps my sweetest memory is of the time that my cousins harmonized on my aunt's favorite hymn, "In the Garden." It was ultimately the song that my cousin Paula's husband Tim sang at my aunt's graveside service.

Now it is the memory of the music and the sing-a-longs at my aunt's bedside that somehow make the memory of her passing a little less painful for me.

This article first appeared on www.opentohope.com

Nessum Dorma

On a Friday in January of 2003, I received a phone call
from my step mom. My dad's sister Shirley had pneumonia.
It was bad, she was in hospice, and could die at any time. I
felt guilty for not having visited her over the past few years.
She had been living in a nursing home in Dayton since she
had a stroke three or four years before. My dad wanted to
drive together to see my Aunt Shirley. I told him that I did
not want to because I did not want to stay all day.

Alone in my car on Saturday morning, I spoke to my
Aunt Shirley. "Aunt Shirley, please don't die before I get
there. I'm on my way."

The hospice was easy to find, and I arrived about
noon. It was a two level brick structure and as I walked in I
could not believe how quiet it was. I was directed to my
aunt's room. My aunt had a private room. Her daughter,
my cousin Sally, was sitting next to her. On the other side
of the bed was my cousin's daughter Kaytee. The last time
I saw my aunt and my cousins was years prior at a high
school graduation party for Kaytee's younger sister Becky.

My aunt was lying on her side with her eyes closed.
Her breathing was slow and steady, as if she were sleeping.
Sally told me that she had been like that for a few days. I
could not believe how different my aunt looked from how I
remembered her. Her natural hair was a soft gray that was

almost blond flowing onto the pillow. She did not have her teeth in so her mouth was withdrawn, as if she just had a bite of lemon. She was a hundred pounds lighter than I remembered her. Sally, who was also a nurse, told me that my aunt was on morphine, which regulated her breathing. She was not in any pain Sally assured me. Sally stood up and offered me her chair. I sat next to my aunt, took her hand and started talking to her. I talked about my cat and my husband and anything I could think of, and I realized that I was so glad to be there. At first there were tears, but soon my cousin and I started talking about my aunt's evil cat, Princess, which she adopted from me in 1985 when my family moved and we could not keep her. Sally commented that all four of her grown children still hated cats because of Princess. Although her breathing did not change, my aunt's mouth moved slightly as if she wanted to chime in.

Later in the day, many relatives came by and it was the first time we had all been in the same room since the Monopoly games during Christmas at Grandma Miles's house in the 1970's. I learned so many stories about my family: an allergy to an anesthetic that I might have, my Aunt Shirley's obsession with Pavarotti, and that my shutterbug tendencies were genetic. My cousin Kaytee was taking pictures of us leaning over our dying aunt. My cousin Jerri Lynn pointed out to our aunt Shirley that all these people are here for her. Although my aunt had not really moved or reacted all day, a small tear formed in the corner of one of her eyes. We knew that she was still with us. We talked about our grandmother's spirituality and her belief in the afterlife. My cousin's daughter Kaytee piped in and told us that she had a pact with her grandmother. My Aunt Shirley had promised that she was going to give Kaytee a sign after she passed away.

By 9:00 at night, my father had come and gone, and I

was still there. A few of us went out to dinner, and I vowed to Sally that I would buy a Pavarotti CD for Aunt Shirley that night.

After dinner, outside of the Outback Steakhouse, in the freezing January weather, I talked with Jerri Lynn, whose own mother, my dad's other living sister, was suffering from Alzheimer's. I told her about Kaytee's pact with Aunt Shirley, and we both lamented that we could not believe that we had not heard from Grandma Miles. I told her that I had gone to see a psychic and she admitted that she had too. Neither of us made contact with Grandma Miles. She told me that she heard from her father's grandmother, in such detail that she knew it was authentic, but it was not what she wanted.

"So, do you think Aunt Shirley will give Kaytee a sign?" she asked me.

"No – I don't." I was shivering but so caught up in the conversation I did not want to go to my car.

"But she promised Kaytee she would."

"I'm sure she intends to now, but what if it is Kaytee's lesson in life to have faith without a sign?" Jerri Lynn and I both looked at each other and smiled. We knew we should heed our own advice. We said our goodbyes and rushed to our cars.

I drove back to the hospice by myself. In the room, Sally and Kaytee were sleeping in the reclining chairs on each side of my aunt's bed. My aunt was in the same position as she was when I left, but her breathing was slower and shallower. Kaytee woke up and smiled. Before I could stop her, she offered me her seat. Sally woke up and greeted me too.

"I brought Pavarotti." I said as I held up Pavarotti's Greatest Hits.

Sally encouraged me to play it, even though it was midnight. I put it in the CD player and we cranked it up. Nessum Dorma resonated through the room. It is fitting that the title translates to *No one sleeps*. Though we received no reaction from my Aunt, we knew that she loved it. Sally, Kaytee, my Aunt Shirley and I enjoyed Pavarotti for the next two hours. We were at peace.

This article first appeared on www.opentohope.com

Waiting for God

My Great Aunt Alice was a reasonably healthy 87 years old. She was spunky. I really thought I would be submitting her picture to the Today show for the Smucker's jar profile when she turned 100. Then one rainy day in April I received a phone call. It was one of those calls where I knew from the caller's initial tone that I was about to hear bad news. Aunt Alice had a sudden brain aneurysm and went into a coma. When I went to visit her, she was not well. Her breathing was labored and the family knew it was close to the end. Her brother, sister and a couple of my cousins were there. We were her closest relatives as she did not have any children. The hospital told us that there was nothing that we could do and they suggested we transfer Aunt Alice to hospice care.

In hospice, the nurse told us that Aunt Alice could hear us and that we should still talk to her. My Great Uncle (her brother) did not really believe the nurse, but he made an effort anyways. He told her he loved her and that he would miss her. I believed that my aunt could still hear me and I whispered to her. I told her I believed everything would be ok, that it was alright for her to go and that I loved her.

Still, for hours we sat there while she was just barely hanging on. Watching. Waiting. Why? We asked, "Why hasn't she passed?" The hospice nurse said sometimes the patient is waiting for someone to come visit. Who could it possibly be? Everyone that could be there was. My cousin Jim was convinced it was his dog P.J., and he decided to drive home to get the dog. Really, Aunt Alice would have been appalled at the thought of a dog in the hospital, but Jim probably needed a break from the situation.

For hours, I sat next to my aunt and held her hand and watched her slowly breath in and out. The nurse would come in periodically to check on my aunt, but there was little change. My back was to the door when I heard a new voice. A woman entered the room and said softly, "Hi. I'm Norma. I'm Alice's minister." We were surprised to see her because none of us had thought to call the church. We forgot that Aunt Alice might want the prayers. Norma then walked over to the bed to check on Aunt Alice. I will never forget that at that very moment when Norma arrived, Aunt Alice stopped breathing. The minister said, "I think she is gone" and started praying for her. The rest of us all looked around at each other, for we suddenly realized Aunt Alice had been waiting for a sign from God.

This article first appeared on www.opentohope.com

Negotiating with God and Dreaming of Chocolate Cake

The first time I met "Gary" we ended up talking for over two hours. He was in his late 60s and had throat cancer, evidenced by a protruding plum-sized tumor on his neck which he covered with turtlenecks. He explained his spiritual beliefs and told me that he was not afraid to die. In fact, when he found himself saying "die" he would correct himself to say "transition." He told me he intended to come back after he died and guide me. I had so much to learn from him and he had so much to teach.

However, as Gary's health declined, he was less excited about the prospect of dying and became rather anxious. Most of our conversations ended up being consumed by practical matters about his medical care. Maslow's hierarchy of needs suggests that you have to take care of basic needs before you can attend to the spiritual, and that is where we ended up – at the bottom of the pyramid talking about shelter and safety.

In what would be the final week of his life, his health really declined and he went into inpatient hospice. His basic needs were being addressed, and suddenly we were back to attending to the spiritual. He would drift in and out of consciousness, sometimes even while standing. While he was "sleeping" he was very physically active with his whole body. Often it was almost like a game of charades as I would try to interpret what he was pantomiming. I saw him eating (baked beans) and I saw him start a car. When he woke up I would ask him what he was experiencing, and he would tell me as much as he could remember.

One time I noticed that he was in conversation and when he woke up I asked, "what were you doing?"

"Negotiating," he said.

"With whom?" I asked.

He shrugged his shoulders indicating he did not know.

I said, "Well, what were you negotiating?"

"They were taking parts of my life and twisting it and making me look at things in a different way."

This intrigued me. "How does that make you feel? Does that make you happy because you're seeing things in a new light?"

His brow furrowed. "No, it doesn't make me happy! They're making me think about things I've been avoiding for 60 years."

Later he would look at me in confusion. He finally told me that he was having trouble distinguishing between worlds. He also said, "I'm having trouble distinguishing between you and my mother."

I must have made a face, because to be mistaken for a woman his mother's age was a little unsettling. He went on to explain, "My mother died when she was old, but she is coming back to me as your age."

I said, "Well, what is she doing?"

"She's trying to ply me with chocolate cake."

During his four day dying process, Gary reported that he saw many loved ones, including his beloved collie, Samantha, who had died last summer. He frequently had dreams of boats, motorcycles and cars. He was definitely planning on taking a trip!

The night before he died, Gary literally tried to sneak out of the facility. I was not there, but apparently he popped his head out the door to his room and tried to make a run for it past the nursing station. Fortunately, the nurses saw him and directed him back to his room. He knew he had somewhere to go and was anxious to get there. He insisted on staying fully dressed and leaving his tennis shoes on until the very end.

I was not at his bedside when he actually died but that did not surprise me – he was always very independent. He waited until I went to get a Diet Coke out of the vending machine. The nurse panicked when she came to find me, but I was not upset. I understood it was his way of downplaying the "transition," which he considered to be a non-event. We don't die, I remembered him telling me.

Though I only knew Gary for three months, the experience of knowing him will stay with me for a lifetime.

This article first appeared on www.opentohope.com

Does Jesus Like Chocolate?

She was staring at the glass of chocolate Ensure. "Annie" did not like chocolate but was so devout in her Catholicism that she did not want to offend Jesus. She looked up at me and asked, "Does Jesus like chocolate?" It was such a funny question and I stifled a laugh, because I knew she was completely serious in her inquiry. Fortunately, I knew the real question behind the question. Will Jesus be mad at me if I do not like chocolate? I smiled and said, "Jesus loves chocolate, but he forgives you if you don't like it."

She stared at the glass, caught up in her indecision between not wanting the chocolate but not wanting to offend Jesus. It was not long before the decision was made for her. Another resident sidled up to the table, grabbed the glass and swallowed it one gulp as if it were a shot of whiskey. He pounded the empty glass down and walked away. Problem solved.

Annie had dementia, and the combination of her dementia and her faith led to all-consuming thoughts of heaven and the afterlife.

"What do you think we'll wear in heaven?" she would ask me.

"I don't know, what do you think?" I would reply. She did not know either.

"How will I get there?" she asked. I told her that maybe Jesus would come to get her. I did not know that for sure, but I have heard more than one story from other hospice workers who had been told by patients that Jesus had come. She liked the idea.

"What do you think heaven will look like?" she would ask. Sometimes she would look at a picture hanging in her room of blue sky and clouds and tell me that she thought *that* is what heaven would look like.

"I hope I go to heaven," she would say every time I saw her.

Other times she would talk about heaven as if she knew something I did not. "We'll see each other again in heaven," she would tell me in a reassuring way.

Annie ended up being on hospice for four years. She never remembered who I was specifically but she recognized my face when I visited. Because her memory was so bad, her family and I would write notes for her reminding her of our visits. I would also write down what we had done during the visit. Usually I would just say that we visited and prayed together. Although she could not remember that we prayed, she found comfort in knowing that she had just prayed when she read the notes.

One time, in the final few months of her life, it occurred to me to write, "God loves you, Annie." She read it aloud and then smiled. She looked up at me and said, "God loves you too, Elizabeth." It the first time in four years that she had spontaneously uttered my name. My jaw dropped. She said, "That is your name, isn't it?" With tears in my eyes, I nodded yes, it is.

What would turn out to be just a few days before she died, I visited her. When I walked in, she said hello and then said, "We've been friends for a long time, haven't we?" I said that we had.

Two days later, I got a phone call that she had suddenly taken a turn for the worse and that she was non-responsive. The next day I went in to see her and said my name. Though her eyes were closed, her eyebrows raised. She looked completely different from just a few days before. She seemed to be in pain as her brow was furrowed. The room was hot and so was she. I put a damp cloth on her forehead and I notified the nurse of her fever. At first I was not sure what to say or do because usually she leads the conversation but then it occurred to me to pray. I started praying the rosary and as I did, I saw her mouth moving along, trying to pray with me. As I prayed the rosary, I saw her face relax and I knew that was what she needed. When I left, she appeared to be resting peacefully. I learned that she died the following day.

I look forward to the day when Annie can tell me for sure whether Jesus likes chocolate.

This article first appeared on www.opentohope.com

Bibliography

Here is a short list of mass market resources that you might find to be helpful if someone you love is dying.

Byock, I. *Dying Well: Peace and Possibilities at the End of Life.* New York: Riverhead Books, 1998.

Callanan, M. & Kelley, P. (1997). *Final Gifts.* New York: Bantam.

Chadwick, G. (2008). *Future Lives.* New York: Sterling.

Halifax, J. (2009). *Being with Dying: Cultivating Compassion and Fearlessness in the Presence of Death.* Boston: Shambala.

Groves, R. & Klauser, H.A. (2009). *The American Book of Living and Dying.* Berkley: Celestial Arts.

MacGregor, T. & MacGregor, R. (2011). *Synchronicity and the Other Side: Your guide to Meaningful Connections with the After Life.* Avon, MA: Adams Media.

Mendoza, M. (2008). *We Do Not Die Alone: "Jesus is Coming to Get me in a White Pickup Truck."* Dahlonega, GA: ICAN.

Moody, R. *Glimpses of Eternity: Sharing a Loved One's Passage from this Life to the Next.* New York: Guideposts, 2010.

O'Donohue, John. (2008). *To Bless the Space Between Us: A Book of Blessings.* New York: Doubleday, 2008.

About the Author

Lizzy Miles is a licensed social worker, hospice volunteer, and a passionate advocate for hospice and end-of-life issues. She has presented her research and experiences with death and dying at national and international grief conferences. She openly admits that she believes in spirit communication and has been blogging about synchronicities and signs from the universe for over seven years at **www.followthesigns.blogspot.com**.

Lizzy lives in Central Ohio with her husband and two cats.